The Light & Darkness of Love

Jenn Murphy

BookLeaf Publishing

India | USA | UK

Presentation by *BookLeaf Publishing*

Web: www.bookleafpub.com

E-mail: info@bookleafpub.com

ISBN: 9789363316140

First edition 2024

I would like to dedicate this book to those who live in darkness, fear or despair.

Love can be a double-edged sword capable of leveling mountains or building kingdoms.

You are not alone.

There is a path forward.

I believe in you.

Believe in yourself.

Keep Going.

ACKNOWLEDGEMENT

I would like to acknowledge all the beautiful new faces and souls I've encountered over the last year. The journey has been long and difficult but I am truly grateful that you stayed with me.
I did not always make that an easy chore. To those that held my hand when I needed it most, I can never repay my debt to you so I will have to pay it forward to future generations. My love is with you always.

To my mother, Yvonne - Talent is in our blood and the abilities and messages I received over the years from you have saved my life on more than one occasion. Thank you for loving me. I hope I've made you proud.

To my sister, Dawn - No one could ask for a better sister than the one I have. Thank you for always being a port in the storm, a smile in the sadness, a laugh when it's needed most. It's a privilege to be one of "the girls."

To my sons - Quin & Jack, you are my heart and my soul. Watching you grow up into the men you have become has brought me the greatest amount of joy a mother could have. I look forward to the future you build and watching it unfold. I love you always.

To my husband - David, words can't describe what I want to say. We've climbed a mountain, you and I. Let's enjoy the air and see what's on the other side. I love you more than you will ever know and always will.

PREFACE

I started writing this collection of poems at the beginning of a dark night of the soul. I had asked God to remove hope from my heart and he did.

For all my bother, God just gave me back the same hope and said "Sorry, I meant for you to have this."

Life, sometimes, isn't kind to those whose hearts are too big and their imaginations too wide but looking for the beauty in others is the only way one can truly rise above.

Some poems in this collection are new, some are old. Some are painful and some are beauty in motion.

I hope you find at least one that resonates with you and make it your own.

My Star

I sometimes pretend you are a star.
A glorious star, burning brightly in the night sky.

Your light radiates for miles around for all the
world to see.

I spend my nights gazing towards the heavens,
bathed in a pale imitation of the heat we once
shared.

The distance is immense.

You drifted so far away I can no longer reach
you.
Do you ever search for me on the ground below?

I whisper sweet nothings to the wind that echoes
back to my broken heart.
I pray my frail voice can find its way to your
soul.
Will we meet again?

I fear you will always remain out of my reach,
glorious star, only to be seen from afar.

Always to remain a step from the arms of the
one who loves you so dear.

I must be content to only gaze upon your beauty
when the sun rests
and lost souls wander the earth with the forlorn.

My love must remain with me.
My faint cries always to fall on deaf ears.

But each night, I will return to slumber in the
warm embrace of your glow
like a moth returning to the flame.

The Life of a Girl

Life is difficult when you're a girl.
You find yourself alone, a lot longing for a
connection to something.

But what?

Don't be too pretty.
Don't be too bold.
Don't be too silly.
Don't be too old.

Sit up straight. Settle down.
Shut your mouth.
You don't need a crown.

Always smile. Be aware.
Apologize to all and never share.

Don't sweat, cry, laugh, eat or drink and most of
all, you mustn't think.

Your hair is too short.
Your clothes are too tight.
You mustn't ever leave the house at night.

You're ugly when you're pretty.
You're mean when you shine.
Nothing is yours; it's always mine.

Take what you're given and smile with grace.
Don't have an opinion or you'll get a smack in
the face.

Follow their lead.
Don't lag too far behind.
If you're told to be there, make sure you're on
time.

Take all of the blame, the guilt, and the shame
and realize,
you're just part of their game.

Keep your legs crossed.
Wash that shit off your face.
They're counting on you to not be a disgrace.

Don't for a minute enjoy a second of life, for
surely it will cause someone, turmoil or strife.

Say please and say thank you and do it with
care,
reputations are wanting, and people may stare.

Remember, you never belong to yourself.

Your mother, your father, your husband, your
kids, your pets, other people, your time's up for
bids.

Go without so others feel good.
You must always do this because they never
would.

Take your feelings and lock them down tight,
push as hard as you can with all of your might.

Don't ask for attention, love, gifts or praise,
people will think you were horribly raised.

You're the help. Don't expect any to come.
It's your duty, you see, there's nowhere to run.

Just ignore the comments or glances.
Ignore the gentlemen and perverted stances.

You mustn't hurt their feelings. It's not their
fault, you see.
Some like your shape.
Some like your hair.
Some like your knees.

You should've covered up.

See, they thought you a whore but covering up
will make them want you all the more.

Don't take a kind word.
You're just leading them on.
Become invisible.
No voice and no song.

Make yourself as small as you can.
Be watchful and protective.
Don't trust any man.

But wait for a prince, a hero, or betrothed
to lock you away and let you grow old.

While he runs to and fro, enjoying his life.
Be proud of your title. He made you his wife.

You had no choice in the matter, you were
picked out and bought like ice cream or cookies,
a craving to scratch until his taste buds had
deadened and his fancy had changed to a
newfangled model.

Something new.
Something strange.

Remember to make sure dinner's on the table.
The kids are in bed.

The dishes are done.
The pets have been fed.

And after he's snoring, tiptoe away for the night
to cry in the darkness and dream of a flight to
anywhere, any place.
Topeka, Paris, or Rome.
Or if you're in luck, the plane will crash on your
home.

A house that's a prison, with warden and gate.
Where your title becomes Queen of the plates,
spoons, cups, pans …..

And as you drift off to sleep, your mind starts to
twirl
because you've been given the life of a girl.

In the Depths of Pain

In the depths of pain, I found you covering your
face from the sun.
I offered you a hand to rise, but the response
there wasn't one.

Cowering in your darkness, I sat down beside
you, intent to wait;
Not sure if our journey would move us forward
to Hell or Heaven's Gate.

The silence while I waited was more than I
could bear.
My heart became so heavy; my lungs struggled
to fill with air.

You thrashed and snarled.
You shrieked and cried.
The prison held you tight.

I laid my head beside the trap and kept watching
through the night.

You couldn't take a moment to open up your
eyes and see that demons vanish and love can
conquer lies.

Did you hear me calling, begging you to rise?
That the bars were made of paper—was that of
no surprise?

I watched you tortured slowly, day and night on
end.
My heart, it hurts so badly.
My knees, they had to bend.

To see a light that's fading from the weight of
others' guilt; a soul, in anguish for a love that no
one ever built.

I would've gladly traded places if it would
release you from your pain,
then you could have continued your journey
further down the lane.

Alas, the world—it isn't designed in such a way.

So, for now, I'll continue sitting and calling to
you,
praying for the day.

Am I Real?

Am I real to you?

Do you see me?

Can you hear the sound of my voice or am I a
ghost to you chained to this existence?

A prop, a show pony, a haven, a mask, did you
once think to stop and to ask?

To trust that I love you?
To let you be mine?

Not to make me a toy that continues to pine to
just be included?

You continue your journeys.
You leave me behind.

After all, you'll fill me in some other time.

Telling me tales of discovery and adventures
galore, while I sit rotting, all alone, on the cold
tile floor.

Lies & Truth

Open the box. Look inside.

All the secrets fall to the floor with a loud bang.

Lies or truths. Does it matter?

The contents are all carelessly tossed in a
tangled pile on the dirty floor.

There's a bit of honesty. Its tag has been torn off.
There's a bit of trust, bent and crushed by the
weight of betrayal.
There's a bit of patience, scuffed beyond repair.
There's a bit of love. Wonder how that got in
there?

Some more pieces:

Laughter, joy, peace, and shame.
Sanity, guilt, grief and blame.

All beaten and strained.

One must untangle the mess, a daunting task.
placing the items back in the box where they
belong.

Never to look again.

I'm sorry, Mr. Piranha

I'm sorry, Mr. Piranha,
I chipped your tooth.
My bones were too hard for such a delicate
mouth to feast.

I'm sorry, Mr. Piranha,
That my heart wasn't a more satisfying meal.
It was far too soft and tender.

I'm sorry, Mr. Piranha,
That my muscles were tough.
I had been running for far too long, you see.

I'm sorry, Mr. Piranha,
That my soul wasn't a tastier meal,
while you were devouring me.

The Person that You Met

I have no forgiveness left to give, my slightest
clean.
I have no anger left to yell, life has moved on.

I have only love left, a small seed with time and
nourishment will bear beautiful fruit.
But who will sit at my table for the feast?

Your invitation was sent; as yet, it goes
unanswered.

"You must find yourself first," you yelled the
last time that we spoke.
The world was out there calling.

I'll set the table and prepare the food. The time
to dine is set.

I wonder if you'll arrive on time with the person
that you met.

A Soliloquy of Silence

Silence is merely the absence of sound,
Words that fall on deaf ears and closed minds,
Tumbling much too quickly to the ground,
But nothingness envelops and binds.

Silence is neither loving or mean.

The snow silences the world while seeds and
flowers sleep.

Come spring, the eye delights in the new shades
of green.
A pause, a slumber, an opportunity for
something meaningful and deep.

Those of nervous dispositions need only speak
to shatter its hold,
With an honest approach and with hearts made
of gold.

Incantation

I am one; I am all.

The last one standing. The last one to fall.

I am the oak, tall and strong.
I am the sky, vast and wondrous.
I am the ocean, deep and calm.
I am the fire, dancing brightly.

My realm was decreed by the seven pillars, the great power, and all will return when their name is called.

My Little Book of Poetry

My little book of poetry was for my amusement,
Not yours.

Your jealousy amazes me.

Anger seeps through the night air—or is it
insecurity?
Who knows the inner workings of your mind?

My little book of poetry was a way for me to
heal.
Not you.

Your jealousy amazes me.

A turn of events to watch as a man willingly
loses himself
to an old state of affairs.

My book of poetry was mine to share.
I will.

Your jealousy amazes me.

My light grows brighter as you try to dim it once
again.

My little book of poetry.
Your jealousy amazes me.

Tempest in a Teapot

A whirl of excitement, energy, rushing madness,
yet the surface is calm.

A smile hides the inner chaos, the hopes, the
fears, all colliding in a symphony of sound.

Injury? Who provides the balm?

Is the storm coming, commencing, passed?

Was its damage slight or enormous?

Who is to say a new day has dawned?
Who is to say the faint sounds of thunder aren't
carried on the sweet breeze of silence?

Storms rage at moments in the smallest of
things.
Large squalls grow as the tiniest of droplets birth
massive wings.

A fragile teapot can withstand all the violence it
was crafted to contain,
but a citadel,

it may collapse when it's touched by the
tempest's coming rain.

The Tongues that Wag

The tongues that wag.
The teeth that bite, seeking nourishment from
another's blood.
How sad their lives must be carelessly tossing
their words about.
Mowing down happiness and truth in their path.

They may think their sins are hidden, but God
sees.

Each falsehood is a stone to sink with jealous
intent.
A path of cobblestone for the malcontent,
creating footholds to rise above their petty
chattering.

The tongues that wag.
The hands that clasp for control and justification
of being nothing more than an empty mouth and
a soul that is lying there, wasting.

As I Walked Today

I went for a morning walk today along the
sidewalks near my home.
There were warm smiles and bright faces. My
feet were graceful and my heart was light.

A voice spoke to me, "Don't stop," offering
words of encouragement, as a sunbeam rested on
my cheek.

We walked the path together.

I went for an afternoon walk today along a
winding forest path. There were brisk winds and
long shadows. My feet were tired and my heart
was burdened.

A soft voice whispered, "Nothing is as it
seems," leaving doubt on my brow.

A fork in the road lay up ahead and I searched
for you among the trees.

I went for an evening walk today between the
weathered stones of my family. There was a chill

in the air, and the light grew dim. My feet were heavy and my heart was cold.

A distant voice whispered, "Let go," and the light faded from my eyes.

I sat in that moment as time stood still and yet passed. There was sadness in the air and darkness had fallen. My feet were frozen and my heart smelled of grief.

The silence was deafening.

I don't think I'll walk anymore.

Always Alone

Come to my shop, said the man, the world has a
beautiful view from upstairs.
I climbed the flights, one, two, three,
After asking the bartender for the key.

I waited, day turned to night, night turned to day.
I waited, anyway.

Always alone.

Come to the shore, said the man, the world is
rich and vibrant.
I watched the scenery fly by,
Birds dancing in a bright blue sky.

I waited, night turned to day, day turned to night
I waited, heart full of fright.

Always alone.

Come to my party, said the man, there'll be
merriment and love.
I raced down the street
Strangers to meet.

I waited, day turned night, night turned to day
I waited, just in the way.

Always alone.

Come to my castle, said the man, I'll make you
my Queen.
I flew in the air, with the clouds at my feet.
My heart skipped a beat.

I waited, night turned to day, day turned to night
I waited, nothing too bright.

Always alone.

Come to my church, said the man, you'll be
worthy then.
I looked up at the cross and sat in my pew.
In the colorful rainbow of the stained glass hue.

I waited, day turned to night, night turned to day
I waited, just in the way.

Always alone.
Come to my meeting, said the man, we'll be
partners then.
I said no. I'll take my path and you go take
yours.
He objected with thunderous roars.

I worked, night turned to day, day turned to
night.
I worked, and there was a bite.

Always alone.

Come to my asylum, said the man, you're crazy
and my reputation's been stained.
My heart broke again as I realized it wasn't
deranged.
A plot for vengeance, a wish for revenge.

I waited in the house that I "stole" with the case
that was brought.
I waited for a fairytale that didn't meant naught.
I waited for a man that wasn't really a thought.
I waited as my mind was thoroughly rot.

Just so he could be happy to leave me,

Always alone.

Being A Gentleman

I prayed for God to rip hope from my heart
and God, being a gentleman, answered my
prayer.

It was dark and painful like the night was
closing in.
I reached for you, but being a gentleman, you
were not there.

I lay there for hours, days, weeks?
The sun and moon, being gentlemen, kept time
of my despair.

I fell slowly through fears and doubts and
shame.
The memories, being gentlemen, haunted me
offering no repair.

In the blackest of that endless night while my
heart was split apart.
God, being a gentleman, touched me and finally
healed my broken heart.

Salvation & Hope

Angels come in many forms.
Their timing, a divine act,
hands of hope and healing.

Wings hidden from sight,
unfurling to bear sorrows of the broken-hearted.

Haiku Quintet

Cop On

Universal message displayed.
Doubt should have run its course now.
Would you please, cop on?

Retrograde

Two bodies spinning
Either direction not known
Journeying through the night sky

Lighthouse

A light shines in the darkness
Unaware of its pull
Lighting the way for the heart.

Gates of Hell

The gates of hell open
Fire flames licking at my feet
And I still walk on

Waiting

I'm still waiting here.
Where did you think I was going?
I always stay put.

Letting Go

The weight of wanting you is crushing me.
My greed will never be sated with friendship
and pleasantries.

There will always be a longing for more.
I can bend and shift just to remain, but my soul
will always want gain.

Love me and only me, and if not, love me
enough to let me go.

If you return, do not return in darkness, shroud
in guilt and shame.
If you return, do not return in desperation, full of
fear and doubt.
If you return, never look at the events of life in
that light again.
If you return, bring a smile and a warm breeze, a
thrill in your heart.
Love is not to be carried or buried in the dark.

Bring your whole self,
the joys, the pains, the mistakes, the wins

If you return, do not feel an obligation, a debt to pay.
If you return, return this time and just stay.

Of these "ifs" I carry in my soul, will you return if I let you go?

What You Taught Me

You taught me that I matter.
Who I am and what I think.

You taught me how to battle,
to stand tall and never shrink.

You taught me how to wrap myself tight, to
protect that beautiful spark of a heart that's
overflowing with love and hidden in the dark.

You taught me to keep going when the fire's hot
and burns.

You taught me to remember myself when the
world rejects and spurns.

You taught me to steal my spine from the things
that people thought, a determination to
overcome and a soul that's never bought.

You taught me to stand proud of myself, the
person I've become.

You taught me about loyalty and you taught me
about home.

You taught me about the ups and downs of life
and the passing of the storm,
family, no matter what, never to conform.

You taught me patience.
You taught me understanding.
You taught me acceptance
And so many things.

But my favorite thing you taught me is that love
really does have wings.

If ever you find yourself looking back feeling
pain or some despair, just remember all you
taught me.

And love the road that got me there.

The Claiming Moon

Claiming moon, continual,
washing souls of all limits,
exposed bare in ritual,
Renewed and emptied spirits.

Brave child of fire aerated,
the universe at bent knee,
both joined and celebrated,
for now; for eternity.

Wonderland

A seeming realm of confusion.

A topsy-turvy roller coaster of thoughts where
midnight skies meet bottomless pits of
nothingness.

A girl is met with a series of doors.

Some wide open,
Some shut tight,
Some ajar,
Some blocked.

She could push with all her might, but still never
open them.
She is trapped in this hallway, frozen in place
waiting for a key to appear.

A sign?

Which door to open and walk through?
Which path leads her home?

Voices advise.

Multiplying and ending in a deafening
crescendo.
Looking up, the world disintegrates into an
ethereal plane of calm.

The choice was made long ago.
Silly girl, she was home all along.